Citizen Scientist

STUDYING INSECTS

IZZI HOWELL

PowerKiDS press
New York

Published in 2023 by The Rosen Publishing Group, Inc.
29 East 21st Street, New York, NY 10010

Copyright © 2020 Wayland, a division of Hachette Children's Group

All rights reserved. No part of this book may be reproduced in any form without permission in writing from the publisher, except by a reviewer.

WARNING
TRY TO AVOID TOUCHING INSECTS. YOU MAY HARM THEM OR THEY MIGHT HURT YOU!

Series Editor: Izzi Howell
Series Designer: Rocket Design (East Anglia) Ltd

Cataloging-in-Publication Data

Names: Howell, Izzi.
Title: Studying insects / Izzi Howell.
Description: New York : PowerKids Press, 2023. | Series: Citizen scientist | Includes glossary and index.
Identifiers: ISBN 9781725338296 (pbk.) | ISBN 9781725338319 (library bound) | ISBN 9781725338302 (6 pack) | ISBN 9781725338326 (ebook)
Subjects: LCSH: Insects--Juvenile literature.
Classification: LCC QL467.2 H767 2023 | DDC 595.7076--dc23

Picture acknowledgements:
Getty: Jirafic 7c, MicrovOne 7b, SimeonVD 14b, jsnyderdesign 15b, mervin07 20, artloct 29b; Shutterstock: penguin_house, designer_an, Magicleaf, vectorOK and Lyudmyla Kharlamova cover, Magicleaf title page, Spreadthesign 4, Elegant Solution 5t, sun7 and Huseyin Altinel 5b, Drogatnev and Maquiladora 6, Elegant Solution 7t, bellflower 8t, BagirovVasif 8b, Kazakova Maryia 9t, Shanvood 9b and 30, LuckyVector 10tl, Vasenina Daria 10tr, Yes - Royalty Free 10bl, Sulee_R 10br, suesse 11, Krissadakorn, Ain Mikail, Cidonia, SLKi and mayrum 12, VectorSun 14t, Studio Photo MH 14c, Jamesbin 15t, Fancy Tapis 16t, Gallinago_media, Silbervogel, RedlineVector, Marie Appert, nikiteev_konstantin and KRIBOX 16b, CloudyStock 17t, Formyline 17c, Artem Twin 17b and 18, NPaveIN 21t, Kazakova Maryia 21b, yukitama, HappyPictures, nexus 7, Iamnee, Spreadthesign, Celana, Nikulina Helen A, Foxyliam, Andrey Vyrypaev and Kazakova Maryia 23t, Park Ji Sun 23b, Hennadii H 24t, Iantapix and Pogaryts'kyy 24b, HappyPictures 25t, Tatyana Pogorelova and burbura 25b, Sabuhi Novruzov, Gnatuyk Lesya, Everilda, Kotkoa, Tatiana Liubimova, ArtDemidova and Kunturtle 26, Timofey Tarakanov 27t, pic0bird 27b, mapush 28, Doloves 29t.
All design elements from Shutterstock.

Manufactured in the United States of America

CPSIA Compliance Information: Batch #CSPK23. For further information contact Rosen Publishing, New York, New York at 1-800-237-9932.

Find us on

CONTENTS

CITIZEN SCIENCE AND INSECTS 4
PROJECT: INSECT OR NOT? 6
HABITATS 8
PROJECT: HABITAT HUNTING 10
PROJECT: MAKE A HABITAT CHOICE CHAMBER 12
LIVING TOGETHER 14
FOOD WEBS 16
PROJECT: LOOKING FOR LADYBUGS 18
LIFE CYCLES 20
PROJECT: TRACK A BUTTERFLY LIFE CYCLE 22
INSECTS AT RISK 24
PROJECT: PLANT A BEE-FRIENDLY GARDEN 26
KEEP IT FAIR 28
GLOSSARY 30
FURTHER INFORMATION 31
INDEX 32

CITIZEN SCIENCE AND INSECTS

Citizen science is a way to help out with scientific research across the world, by taking part in observations and submitting data. Working as citizen scientists, we can observe insects to see how they live and how we can protect their habitats.

True insects are small invertebrates, or animals without a backbone, such as bees and butterflies.

True insects have ...

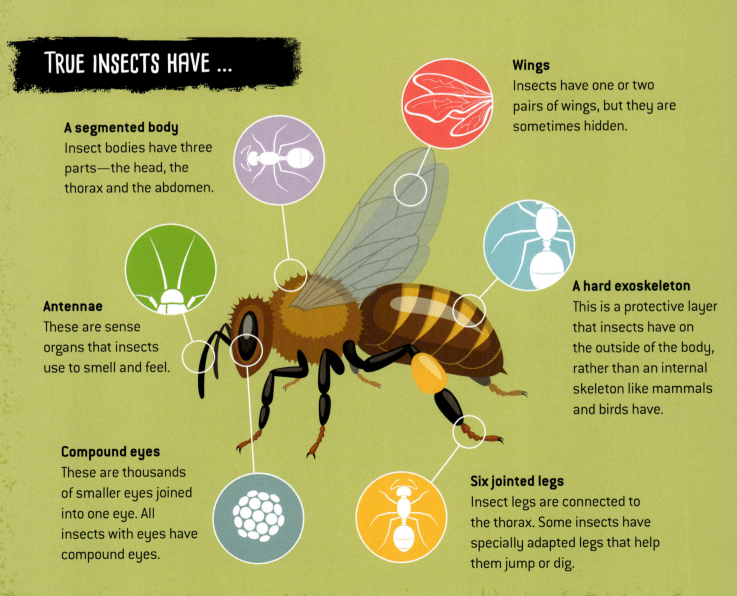

Wings
Insects have one or two pairs of wings, but they are sometimes hidden.

A segmented body
Insect bodies have three parts—the head, the thorax and the abdomen.

A hard exoskeleton
This is a protective layer that insects have on the outside of the body, rather than an internal skeleton like mammals and birds have.

Antennae
These are sense organs that insects use to smell and feel.

Compound eyes
These are thousands of smaller eyes joined into one eye. All insects with eyes have compound eyes.

Six jointed legs
Insect legs are connected to the thorax. Some insects have specially adapted legs that help them jump or dig.

TYPES OF INSECTS

Dragonflies and damselflies
Both species are similar, with a long, thin body. They have two pairs of transparent wings.

Bees, wasps and ants
Many of these species can sting if attacked. Bees and wasps have yellow stripes to warn predators that they sting. They have a narrow waist.

Beetles
Beetles have two pairs of wings. The front pair is hardened and covers the back of the beetle. The back wings are used for flying and remain folded under the front wings when not in use.

Crickets and grasshoppers
They use their powerful back legs for jumping. They only eat plants.

Butterflies and moths
Butterflies tend to have brighter colors than moths. Butterflies are active during the day, while moths are often nocturnal. They both eat through a proboscis—a long tube used for sucking.

Flies
Flies fly with one pair of wings. They also have a small set of wing-like structures that they use for balance. They usually have a mouth for biting and sucking.

NOT REALLY AN INSECT

We often use the word "insect" to describe animals that aren't technically insects, such as snails and spiders. These animals are small invertebrates, but they don't have the right body type or number of legs to be true insects. Some people use the words "bugs" or "creepy-crawlies" for these animals instead.

creepy-crawlies

Around **1 MILLION** different species of insect have been identified so far, and scientists are discovering more all the time.

PROJECT

INSECT OR NOT?

Track down bugs in your local area. Use observation containers to get a closer look at their incredible bodies and decide whether or not they are true insects!

This project can be done almost anywhere—a school playground, a park, a forest, or anywhere else small animals can be found. Explore your surroundings until you find a bug. Catch it in a plastic insect observation container or a glass jar with a lid.

YOU WILL NEED:

paper

a pen

a jar

//// BE CAREFUL ////

Be very careful not to hurt the animal while placing it in the container. If the bug flies, let it fly in. If it walks, place the container nearby and encourage it to walk in, or scoop it in gently with a leaf. Try to avoid touching it if possible.

Observe the bug inside the container. Take note of the number of legs and body segments, the size and shape of its wings and any other important details. Write down your observations and follow the checklist below to decide if it's a true insect or not.

Bug	Observations	True insect?	
ladybug	round body	yes	
	three body segments		
	six legs		
	hidden wings		
	red with black spots		
woodlouse (potato bug or roly-poly)	gray, segmented exoskeleton	no	
	seven pairs of legs		
	antennae		
mosquito	slim body	yes	
	three body segments		
	six legs		
	long antennae		
	proboscis		

INSECT CHECKLIST

Does it have six legs?
Does it have wings?
Does it have three segments?

If your bug ticks off all of these points, it's a true insect! If not, it's a different type of invertebrate.

When you have finished, release your bug where you found it. Repeat with several other types of bugs.

GET INVOLVED!

Use an insect identification guide to figure out the exact species you have found, rather than just "fly" or "beetle." If you find any bugs that aren't insects, try to find out the scientific name of the group they do belong to.

HABITATS

Insects and other bugs can be found everywhere—on plants, in soil, and in water. They are even found in places we'd rather not find them, such as inside our homes.

Microhabitats

Insects can be found in many different specific locations within a habitat. These locations are known as microhabitats. Microhabitats include on flowers, on walls and under stones.

Hiding away

Insects and other bugs, such as beetles and centipedes, like to hide away in dark, damp places, including under logs and dead leaves. They eat the decomposing remains of plants. They play an important role in the ecosystem, helping to clear and recycle this matter away and stop it from building up.

Warm spots

Insects are cold blooded, which means they can't control their body temperature. They depend on their surroundings to warm up or cool down. For this reason, insects sometimes rest in warm spots on walls, windowsills, or fences to raise their body temperature.

Water insects

Many insects can be found in and around fresh water. The young of some insects, such as dragonflies and mosquitoes, hatch and live in water. Adult dragonflies often live near water as well. Pond skaters can balance on the surface of water, while diving beetles dive deep to find prey such as other water insects, tadpoles, and even small fish.

At home

Spiders, mosquitoes, and flies are all often found in buildings. This can be a problem for the people who live there. Female mosquitos bite humans to get nutrients from their blood to produce eggs. Flies land on food and can spread germs. However, spiders can be helpful. They feed on other bugs, such as flies, so they keep homes free of other pests.

Fleas live on cats and dogs and drink their blood. Fleas don't live on humans, but they will bite them if they are hungry.

PROJECT

HABITAT HUNTING

Explore your local area and discover the insects and bugs that live in different microhabitats.

Choose three different microhabitats (look back on pages 8–9 for inspiration). They could be on a plant, under dead leaves, on an outdoor wall, or inside your home.

Spend 10 minutes examining each microhabitat for the species that live there. Use an identification guide to help you identify any unknown species.

Keep a tally of the different species you spot in each microhabitat and draw a table to present your data. Then use the Microsoft Excel program to present your data as a bar chart.

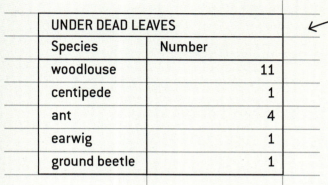

UNDER DEAD LEAVES	
Species	Number
woodlouse	11
centipede	1
ant	4
earwig	1
ground beetle	1

First, copy your data for each habitat into a spreadsheet. It should look something like this.

Next, select all the cells that contain data and click the 'Charts' button. Choose the 'Bar' option. This will create a bar chart from your data.

GET INVOLVED!

Ask your science teacher to make this a class activity. Together, your class can look at all the data and figure out where each insect is most likely to be found. The more data an experiment has, the more accurate the results will be.

PROJECT

MAKE A HABITAT CHOICE CHAMBER

Use choice chambers to find out what kind of conditions woodlice prefer. Each choice chamber is divided into two different conditions—dark or light, and damp or dry. The part the woodlice move into is the one they prefer.

Before you begin your experiment, make a prediction. Which conditions do you think the woodlice will prefer? Use any information that you already know about woodlice to make your prediction. Use the Habitat Hunting activity (see pages 10–11) to track down woodlice.

YOU WILL NEED:

a collection container with a lid, such as a jar

soil and dead leaves

5—10 woodlice

2 clear containers with clear lids

paper towels

black paper

scissors

tape

//// WARNING ////
BE CAREFUL HANDLING SCISSORS!

Place some soil and dead leaves in your collection container to keep the woodlice happy while they are being transported. Collect 5–10 woodlice in the container by allowing them to walk in or gently scooping them in with a leaf.

Prepare your first choice chamber by dampening a paper towel and placing it in half of one of the containers. Fold it if necessary to make it fit. Add your woodlice to the container and close the lid. Leave for five minutes. Check back and see which side of the container the woodlice are gathered in—damp or dry? Make a note of your results.

Prepare your second choice chamber. Take the lid of the second container and cut a piece of black paper to cover half of it. Stick the paper to the lid with tape. Repeat your experiment by placing the woodlice in the container, closing the lid, and leaving for five minutes. Check back to see where the woodlice are—on the dark side or the light side? Make a note of your results.

When you've finished your experiment, place the woodlice back in the collection container and release them where you found them. Then look back at your results and think about what they show you. Was your prediction correct?

TRY IT!

Repeat the experiment with some other bugs. Are the results the same? You could also change the conditions, such as using two different kinds of soil or leaves. However, make sure you don't test any conditions that would hurt the bugs.

LIVING TOGETHER

Some species of bees, wasps, and ants are social and live together in colonies. Each insect has its own role within the colony.

Nests

Social insects live together in nests. Ants nest in underground tunnels or in trees. Bees also build their nests in trees or in caves. We encourage bee colonies to nest in manmade hives so that we can collect their honey.

90% of bees don't live in colonies. They are solitary and live on their own.

Reproduction

The queen is the largest female and the most important insect in the colony. She is the mother of most of the colony, as only she can reproduce. Her only job is to lay eggs. New insects for the colony hatch from these eggs.

queen

drone (male bee)

worker (female bee)

Workers

The workers in a colony perform special tasks, such as finding food, repairing the nest, or feeding the young. Some worker ants are responsible for defending the nest. They are known as soldier ants and are usually female.

Communication

Social insects need to communicate with each other so they know what's going on in the nest. Honeybees communicate through dance. Ants touch antennae to recognize each other through scent. They also leave scent trails to and from food sources so other ants can follow them.

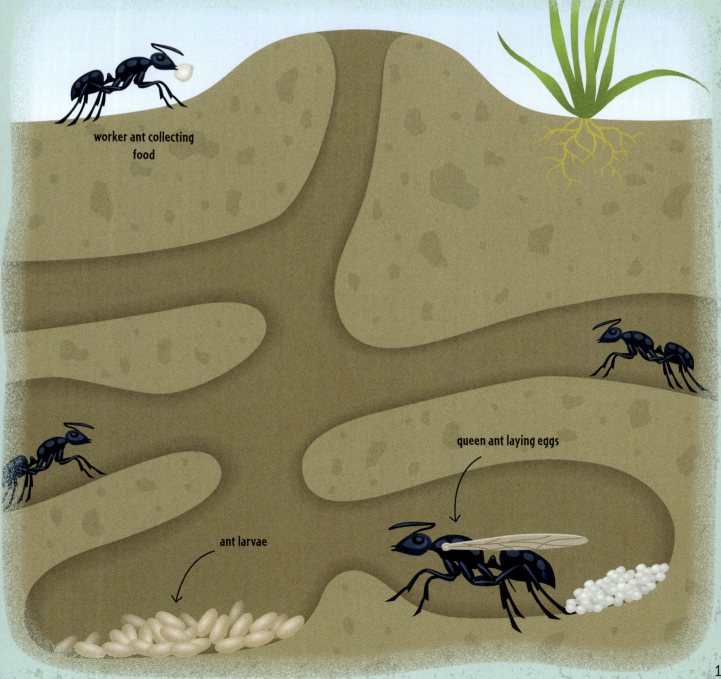

worker ant collecting food

queen ant laying eggs

ant larvae

FOOD WEBS

We use food webs to show where plants and animals get their energy from in an ecosystem. Plants use energy from the sun to make their own food. Animals eat plants or other animals for food.

PREDATORS AND PREY

Predators are animals that eat other animals for food. The animals they eat are called prey. Insects are often the prey of larger animals.

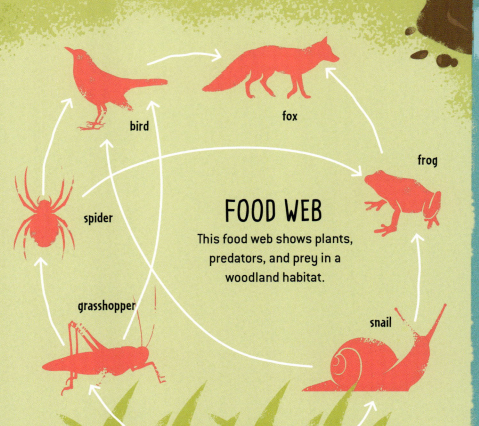

FOOD WEB

This food web shows plants, predators, and prey in a woodland habitat.

POPULATION CHANGES

If the population of one part of the food web changes, it affects the other species in the ecosystem. For example, snails and grasshoppers both eat grass. If the snail population increases, there will be less grass for the grasshoppers. Some grasshoppers will starve and die. Other species further up the food web that depend on grasshoppers for food, such as spiders, will struggle to find food as a result.

INVASIVE SPECIES

Food webs are also affected by new species that settle in an ecosystem. They are called invasive species because they eat the same things and live in the same places as the species that are native, or found naturally, in that ecosystem. This makes it harder for the native species to survive.

HARLEQUIN LADYBUGS

A type of insect called the Harlequin ladybug or Asian lady beetle has been affecting ladybug populations around the world. The Harlequin ladybug was introduced deliberately to Europe and the United States to eat small bugs called aphids that damaged crops. They are now considered an invasive species in these places.

COMPETITION

The arrival of invasive species means less food to go around. Harlequin ladybugs feed on the aphids that are native ladybugs' main food source. They also act as new predators in the ecosystem, eating the larvae of other ladybugs. Native ladybug populations have decreased since the arrival of Harlequin ladybugs.

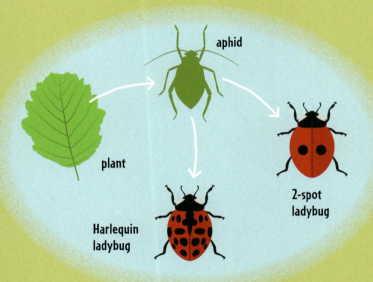

2004

44% decrease in population of the native two-spot ladybug since the arrival of the Harlequin ladybug in the UK in 2004

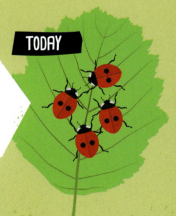

TODAY

PROJECT

LOOKING FOR LADYBUGS

Go on a ladybug hunt and count how many different species you can spot! Are there still native ladybugs in your local area or have invasive species taken over?

Go to a park, garden, or other wooded area. It's best to do this project in spring or summer because many ladybugs hibernate in the winter. Ladybugs are often found on green, leafy plants and trees, but take a look in as many areas as possible. You might want to use a magnifying glass if you have one.

2-spot ladybug • 7-spot ladybug • Harlequin ladybug • 14-spot ladybug
pine ladybug • orange ladybug • convergent ladybug • 9-spot ladybug

When you find a ladybug, identify it using this guide. If you're not sure which type of ladybug it is, check in a book or look online. Draw a picture or take a photo to help you remember what it looks like.

Draw a table to keep track of the number of each species of ladybug that you find. Then, use the Microsoft Excel program to present your data in a circular pie chart. Each species represents a different section of the pie.

Species	Number seen
2-spot ladybug	2
7-spot ladybug	3
Harlequin ladybug	5
pine ladybug	1
14-spot ladybug	1

First, copy your data into a spreadsheet. It should look something like this.

Next, select all the cells that contain data and click the 'Charts' button. Choose the 'Pie' option. This will create a pie chart from your data.

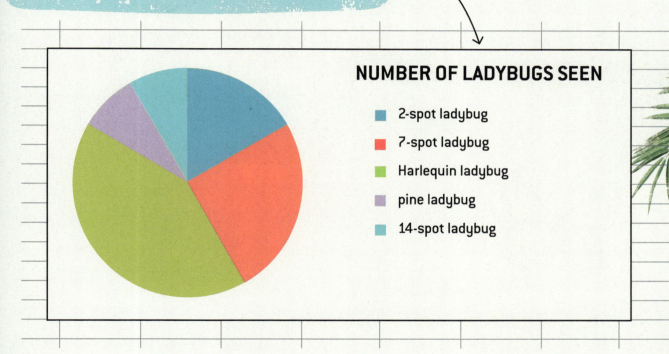

NUMBER OF LADYBUGS SEEN
- 2-spot ladybug
- 7-spot ladybug
- Harlequin ladybug
- pine ladybug
- 14-spot ladybug

GET INVOLVED!
People across the world are hunting for ladybugs to see which species are the most common. Add your data to the survey at www.lostladybug.org.

LIFE CYCLES

All insects hatch from eggs. After that, different types of insects go through different life cycles.

Metamorphosis

Some insects go through a stage in their life cycle called metamorphosis. Their body is totally rebuilt, rather than growing larger over time. This happens to insects such as butterflies, bees, ants, and wasps.

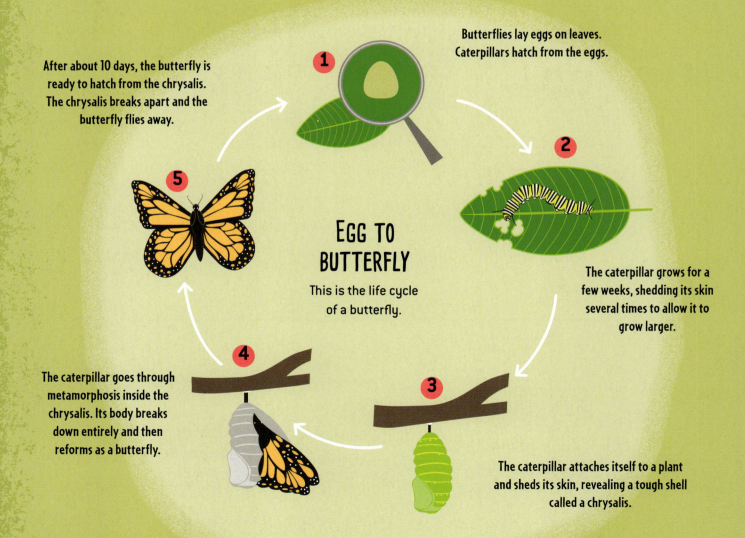

Egg to Butterfly
This is the life cycle of a butterfly.

1. Butterflies lay eggs on leaves. Caterpillars hatch from the eggs.
2. The caterpillar grows for a few weeks, shedding its skin several times to allow it to grow larger.
3. The caterpillar attaches itself to a plant and sheds its skin, revealing a tough shell called a chrysalis.
4. The caterpillar goes through metamorphosis inside the chrysalis. Its body breaks down entirely and then reforms as a butterfly.
5. After about 10 days, the butterfly is ready to hatch from the chrysalis. The chrysalis breaks apart and the butterfly flies away.

Caterpillars

Caterpillars have to eat a lot of plants so they have enough energy to go through metamorphosis. However, they can't fly, so it is easy for predators to find and eat them. Caterpillars use different strategies to avoid being eaten, including green or brown camouflage to blend in with plants, releasing substances that smell bad, or being brightly coloured, as this warns predators that they might be poisonous.

Changing shape

Some insects, such as grasshoppers, crickets, and dragonflies, don't form a chrysalis to go through full metamorphosis. Instead, they shed their skin as they grow, which is called incomplete metamorphosis. Each time they lose their skin, they change shape a little bit and develop adult features, such as wings.

Egg to dragonfly

Young dragonfly larvae hatch in the water. They live for several years (most of their lives) in the water, where they are known as nymphs. They come out of the water when they are ready to shed their skin and take their adult form with wings to fly.

PROJECT

TRACK A BUTTERFLY LIFE CYCLE

Insect life cycles are going on all around you, but you may never have noticed! Track the life cycle of butterflies and create a fact file to record information about eggs, caterpillars, chrysalises, and butterflies. It's best to do this research in spring or summer, when butterflies are most active.

Start by making your fact file. Divide a piece of paper into four sections, one for each stage in a butterfly's life cycle. This is where you'll record all of your observations.

Egg	Caterpillar
Where? When? Which species? Draw a picture	Where? When? Which species? Draw a picture
Chrysalis	Butterfly
Where? When? Which species? Draw a picture	Where? When? Which species? Draw a picture

//// WARNING ////
DO NOT DISTURB OR TOUCH ANY EGGS, CATERPILLARS, CHRYSALISES, OR BUTTERFLIES THAT YOU FIND.

Different butterfly species lay their eggs on different types of plant. Their caterpillars eat this plant once they have hatched. Look closely, since butterfly eggs are small and can be quite hard to spot.

cabbage white on plants in the cabbage family

comma butterfly on nettles and some types of trees, such as elms and willows

swallowtail butterfly on plants in the carrot family

monarch on milkweed plants

peacock butterfly on stinging nettles

Once you've found butterfly eggs, finding caterpillars will be easy because most stay on or around the plant that they hatch on. Take note of where you found the eggs and check back over the next few days or weeks until you spot caterpillars.

Around two weeks after you spot the caterpillars, they'll start forming their chrysalises. These can be tricky to spot; look around the plants where the caterpillars live, under branches and leaves. Be very careful not to damage any chrysalises or knock them off the plant.

Many butterflies are colorful and eye-catching, so they should be easy to spot! Look near flowering plants for butterflies drinking nectar or butterflies laying eggs on plants. If you spot a butterfly laying eggs, make a note of the location and track the life cycle of its young.

GET INVOLVED!

Share your research with other people by uploading the butterflies you spot to the Big Butterfly Count at www.bigbutterflycount.org (UK) or the Butterflies and Moths of North America project at www.butterfliesandmoths.org (USA).

INSECTS AT RISK

Insect populations are under threat because of human activity. Although they are small, insects are a very important part of natural ecosystems. Losing them has a serious effect on the entire natural world.

Pesticides

Insects can have a negative impact on farms, since they eat and damage crops. Many farmers use pesticides to kill insects and protect their crops. However, pesticides kill any nearby insects, not just those that eat the crops. Organic farmers grow crops without the use of pesticides, which is much better for insect populations.

Habitat loss

Many wild insect habitats are being cleared so new homes, businesses, and roads can be built on the land. When people "clean up" wild areas through processes such as deforestation, they destroy important insect microhabitats, such as old logs and wildflowers. People sometimes plant new plants in these areas that don't provide the food and shelter that insects need.

Climate change

Global warming is increasing the average temperature on Earth and affecting weather patterns. This means that plants are flowering and producing fruit earlier than normal. Insects that depend on pollen and nectar go hungry and can die later in the season when flowers and fruit disappear too soon.

Pollination

Decreasing insect populations puts crops at risk. Insects pollinate plants when they land on flowers to drink nectar. Without insects pollinating these plants, flowers would not be fertilized and no fruit or seeds would develop. This would affect many crops that we grow for food as well as wild plants, disrupting entire ecosystems.

90%
of the food eaten around the world comes from plants pollinated by bees.

PROJECT

PLANT A BEE-FRIENDLY GARDEN

Some bee species are disappearing because their food sources, such as wildflowers, are being destroyed. Help the bees by planting a bee-friendly garden and track which bees it attracts!

Different species flower at different times, providing food for bees throughout the year.

Spring
apple blossom, crocus

Summer
chive flowers, lavender

Autumn
sage flowers, honeysuckle

Winter
aconite, snowdrops

Find a space for your bee-friendly plants. It could be your school playground, a garden, or a balcony. If you don't have space to plant anything, you could look for places where these plants already grow and track the bees that visit them.

Try to plant one bee-friendly plant for every season. Follow the instructions on the seed or bulb packet. You may need to plant them at different times throughout the year.

When the plant is flowering, observe it for 10 minutes. Count how many bees visit and keep a tally. Which flowers are the most popular with bees? Do any other insects, such as butterflies, visit these flowers?

Test your observational skills by using an insect observation guide to figure out the species of bee you spot. Count how many of each bee species visit the flower. Are some flowers more popular with some species than others?

TRY IT!

Try planting other species of flowering plant. Are these species popular with bees or other species of insect? Bees also need water to drink, so keep a bowl of rainwater near your plants.

KEEP IT FAIR

All of the experiments in this book will help you to learn more about insects in your local area and how to keep them safe. However, it's important for you to make your experiments fair. If you don't control the different elements of an experiment, the results won't be accurate.

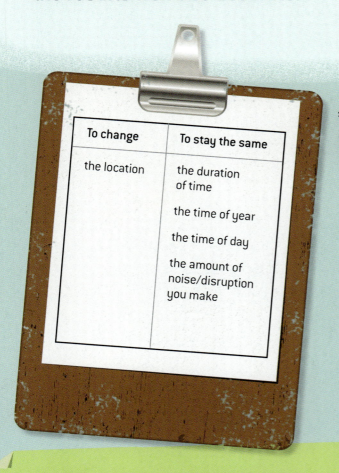

To change	To stay the same
the location	the duration of time
	the time of year
	the time of day
	the amount of noise/disruption you make

VARIABLES

There are lots of elements in experiments. These are called the variables. To make an experiment a fair test, you can only change one variable at a time. All other variables have to stay the same. For example, in the habitat project on pages 10–11, the only variable you are changing is the location. Everything else should stay the same.

INACCURATE RESULTS

If you have more than one variable, you won't know which one has affected your results. For example, if you visited some habitats in summer and some in winter, you wouldn't know if the number of insects was because of the habitat or because of the season. This makes your research invalid.

PLAN AHEAD

It's important to plan how you will make your experiment fair before you begin. This helps keep the variables the same throughout. Write down important details, such as lengths of time, so you don't forget.

OVER TO YOU!

When you've finished the projects in this book, why not make up your own?

First, you need to think of an idea that you want to test. This is called the hypothesis. For example,

> "I THINK THAT SMALL INSECTS PREFER TO VISIT SMALL FLOWERS."

Next, think about your variables. What will you keep the same and what will you change?

Then, carry out your experiment. You should repeat it a few times to make sure your results aren't unusual. Present your ideas using one of the graphs from the book. Finally, use your results to come up with a conclusion. What do the results show you? Was your hypothesis right or wrong?

GLOSSARY

antennae: Long, thin sense organs found on the head of an insect.

camouflage: Having a color or pattern that is similar to the surroundings so it is difficult to see.

chrysalis: The stage of development of a moth or butterfly in which the animal changes its form inside a hard shell.

colony: A group of the same species of animals that live together.

conclusion: The opinion you have after finding out all the information about something.

decompose: To break down

deforestation: Cutting down all the trees in an area.

ecosystem: All the living things in an area.

exoskeleton: A hard outer layer that supports and protects the body of an invertebrate.

hypothesis: An idea that needs to be tested.

invertebrate: An animal without a backbone, such as an insect, crab or worm.

larva: The young of an insect that has not yet reached its adult form.

metamorphosis: The process in which insect larvae change into their adult form.

microhabitat: A small habitat, such as the bark of a tree, found within a larger habitat.

nymph: A dragonfly or damselfly larva.

pesticide: A chemical used to kill unwanted animals or plants.

pollinate: To transfer pollen from one part of a plant to another, which fertilizes the flower.

predator: An animal that kills and eats other animals.

prey: An animal that is hunted and killed by other animals.

proboscis: A long tube that butterflies use for sucking.

species: A group of animals or plants with the same characteristics.

tally: A running total.

variable: An element in an experiment that can change.

FURTHER INFORMATION

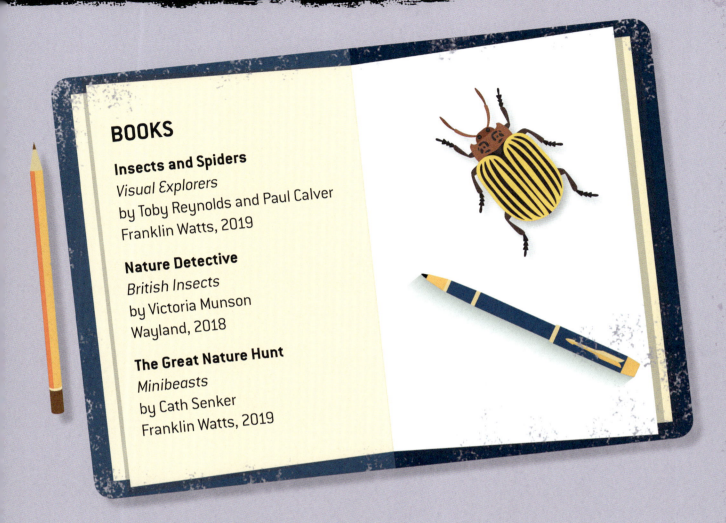

BOOKS

Insects and Spiders
Visual Explorers
by Toby Reynolds and Paul Calver
Franklin Watts, 2019

Nature Detective
British Insects
by Victoria Munson
Wayland, 2018

The Great Nature Hunt
Minibeasts
by Cath Senker
Franklin Watts, 2019

WEBSITES

www.natgeokids.com/uk/discover/animals/insects/15-facts-about-bug
Discover some amazing facts about insects and other bugs.

thekidshouldseethis.com/post/a-ladybug-ladybird-life-cycle-time-laps
Watch a time-lapse video of the life cycle of a ladybug, which is called a ladybird in the United Kingdom (UK).

www.ducksters.com/animals/bugs.php
Learn more about insects and spiders.

INDEX

antennae 4, 15
ants 5, 14, 15, 20

bar charts 11
bees 4, 5, 14, 15, 20, 25, 26, 27
bugs 5, 6, 7, 8, 9, 10, 11, 13
butterflies 4, 5, 20, 22, 23

colonies 14–15

dragonflies 5, 9, 21

eggs 9, 14, 15, 20, 21, 22, 23

fair experiments 28–29
flies 5, 9
food webs 16–17

habitats 8–9, 10, 11, 12, 13, 24

invasive species 17, 18

ladybugs 17, 18, 19

life cycles 20–21, 22, 23

nests 14, 15

pie charts 19
plants 5, 8, 9, 10, 16, 17, 20, 21, 23, 24, 25, 26, 27
pollination 25
projects 6–7, 10–11, 12–13, 18–19, 22–23, 26–27

threats 24–25

variables 28, 29

wasps 5, 14, 20